Wally Gilbert

Broken Image

An Exhibition

at

Viridian Artists

February 2nd to February 21st, 2016

548 West 28th Street
New York, NY

Wally Gilbert continues exploring the microcosmic possibilities of the fragment. In large digital prints on aluminum, the artist creates novel superpositions in brilliant colors. These new, fresh images are still fragments that embody the whole, as the artist has often said of his work.

In the "Broken City" images one can still see the echo of the shapes of buildings and windows even through an extreme transformation. The same can be said of the "Broken Tree" which seems to implode on the surface with a burst of branches that appear to be coming from a hot core surrounded by darkness. Complex recreations of forms and luminous color transformations abound in these works.

In the early 2000's, Nobel Laureate Wally Gilbert started pursuing photography on a professional level. Since then, he has had over 50 solo exhibitions around the world.

As in past exhibitions, Gilbert continues his fascination with transforming images on the computer experimenting with color and other digital effects. He pushes colors to their extreme, sometimes to express the psychological pain of the artistic process, sometimes to explore through color transformations, how we see objects.

In his first exhibit at Viridian in 2006, "The Norblin Project", Gilbert explored and documented an ancient and abandoned factory in Poland. About the works in that show, Ed McCormack in Gallery & Studio said "For Gilbert, the continued exploration of the fragments of reality particularly via the computer and creating strategies to provoke accidents ... inspire the search for and evolution of the next image."

In his solo "Stillness & Motion" in 2008 the images were derived from his travels. In the "Squares and Triangles" exhibit at Viridian in 2011, the critic Peter Frank said "Gilbert ... systematically unfolds entirely unassuming shapes into elaborate scintillations."

The images in his 2013 show "New Black & White Images" exploited the play of natural light across objects to produce haunting results without color, but in his 2014 exhibition, "Transformations", his images again glowed with color driven to full saturation creating new and strange interactions, until they became -- in the artist's words -- "abstract meditations".

In his previous career as scientist, Gilbert was awarded a Nobel Prize in 1980 for his landmark work in DNA gene sequencing. As a scientist, he examined the world in its smallest details, but now through his photography, he makes the small huge to reveal the beauty that he sees in the world.

Vernita Nemec   Chelsea, NY

Catalogue of Images

Facing Page

Large Images

Small Images

Black and White Images

60" x 40" Images

Broken City #6

2016

60" x40"

Printed on Aluminum, edition of 5

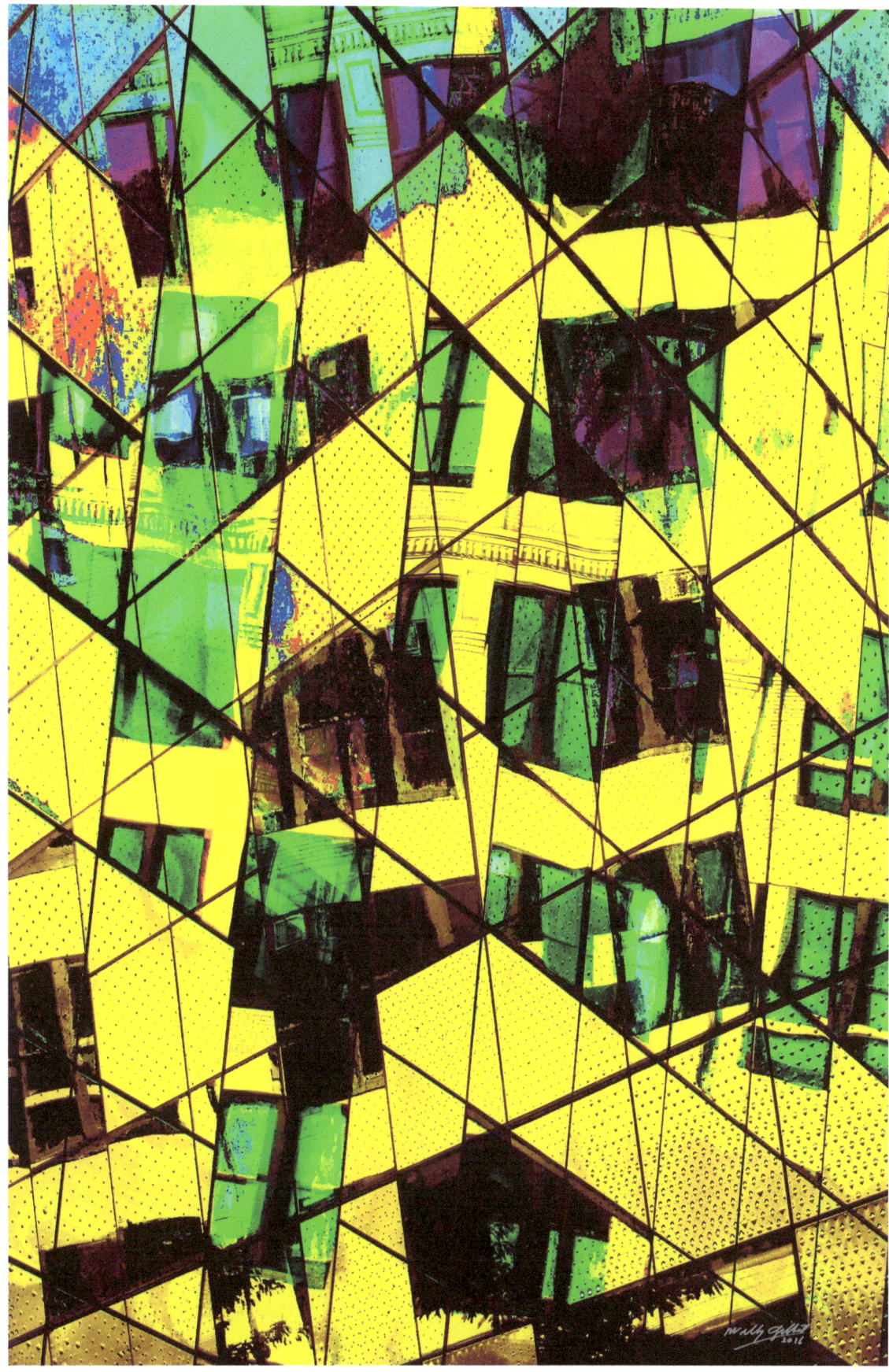

13

Reflections – Red

2015

60" x40"

Printed on Aluminum, edition of 5

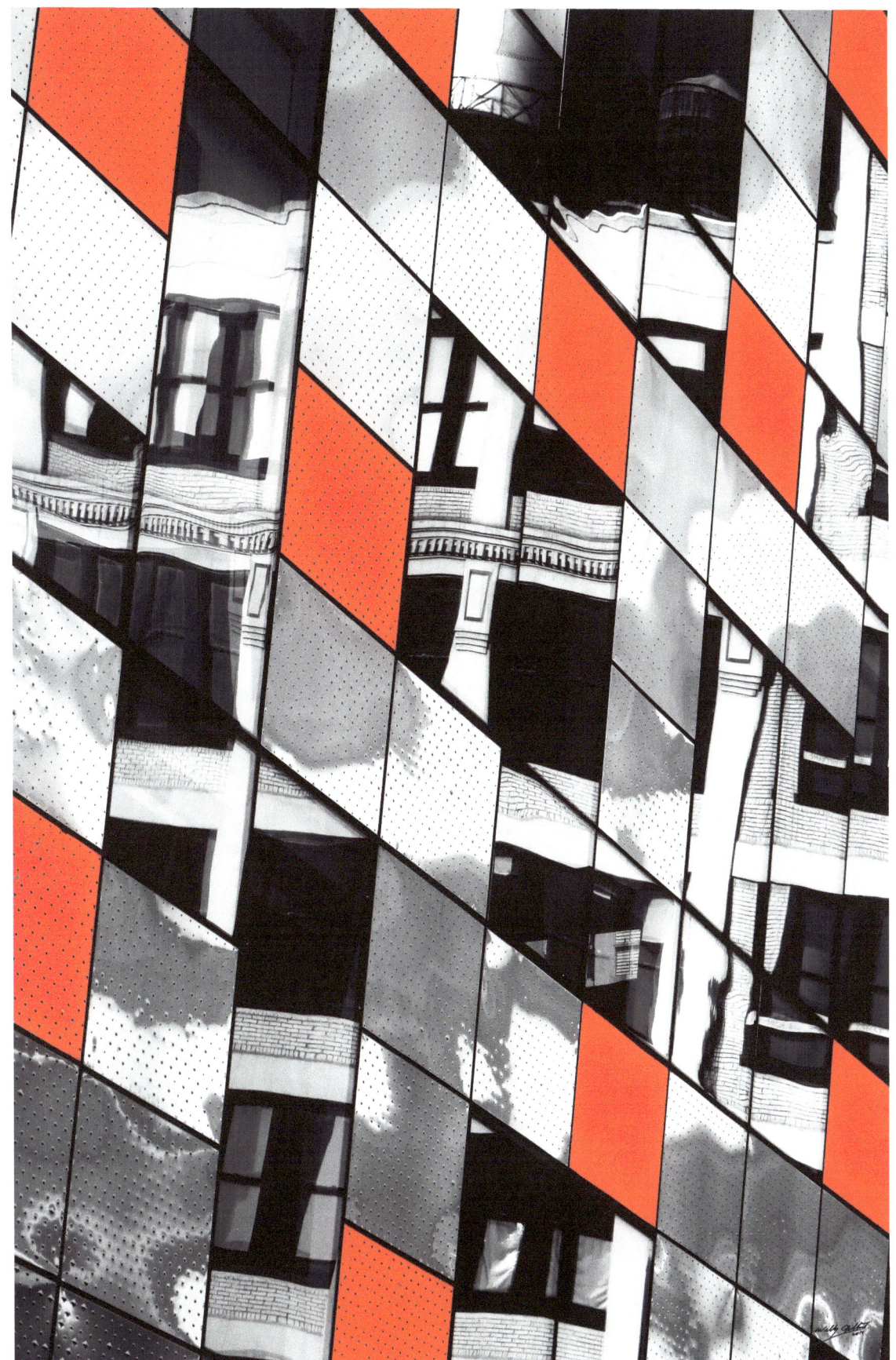

Doors to Nowhere

2015

60" x 40"

Printed on Aluminum, edition of 5

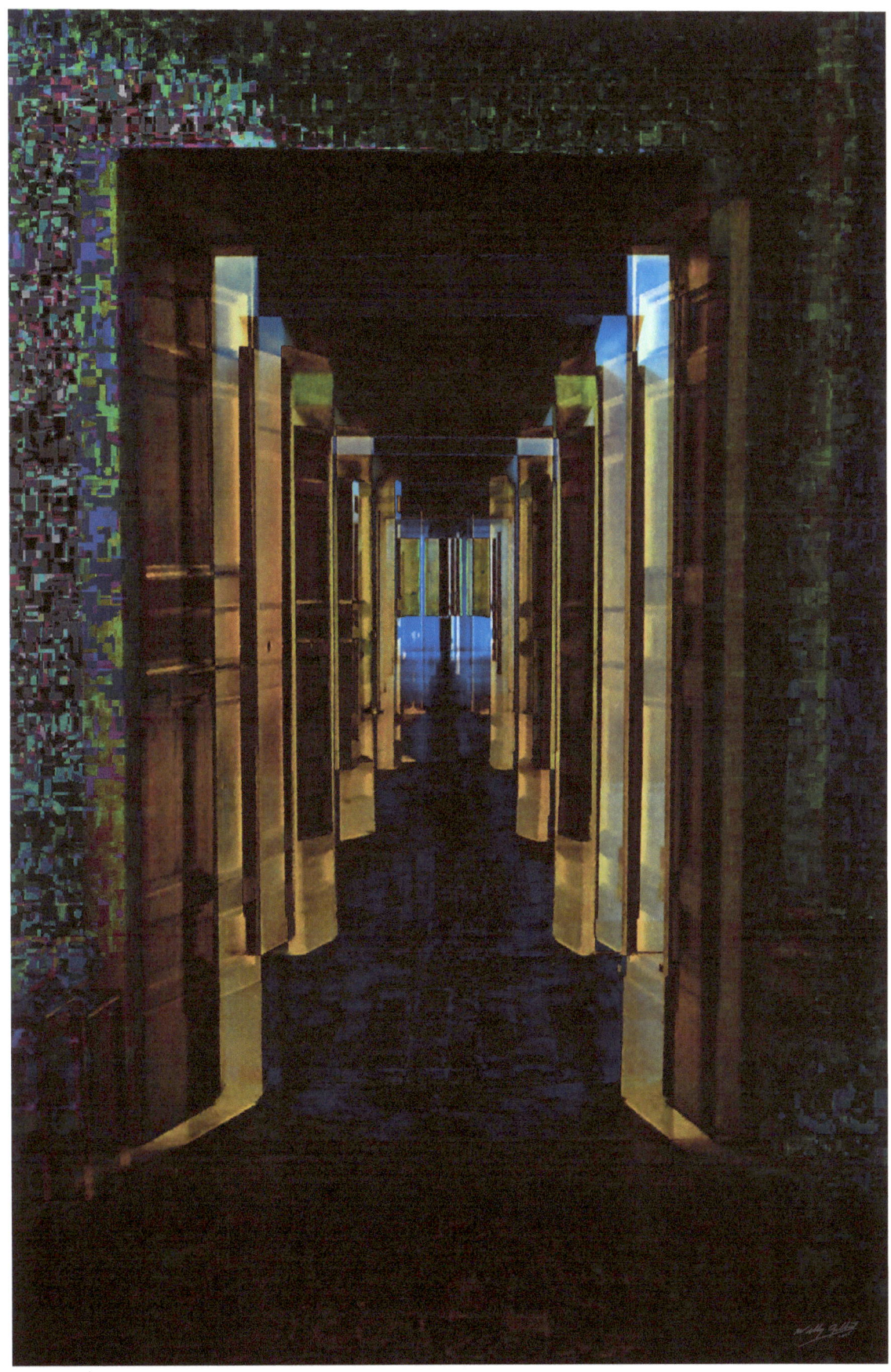

Sequences Reveal

2015

60" x 40"

Printed on Aluminum, edition of 5

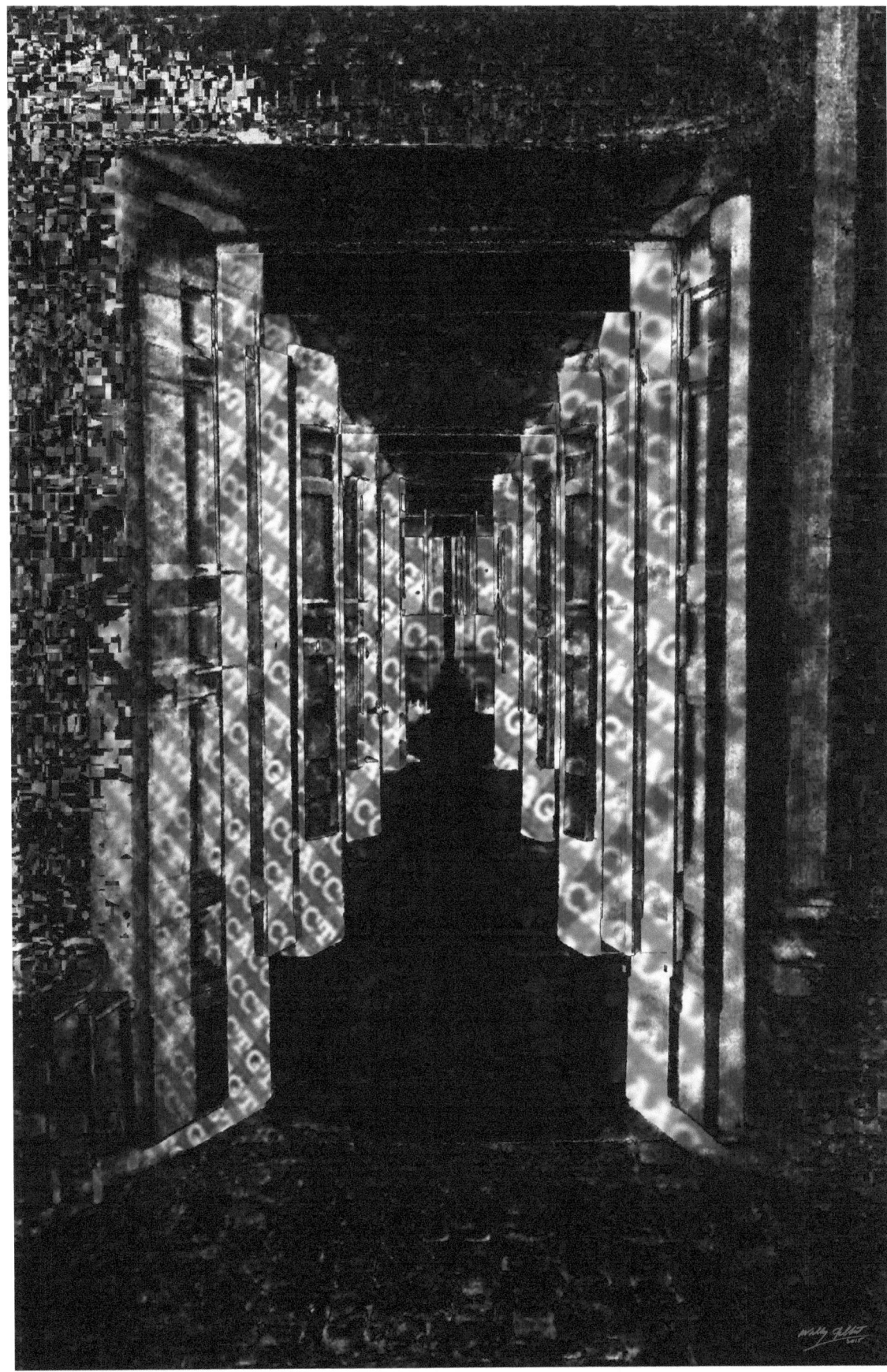

Night Trees

2016

60" x40"

Printed on Aluminum, edition of 5

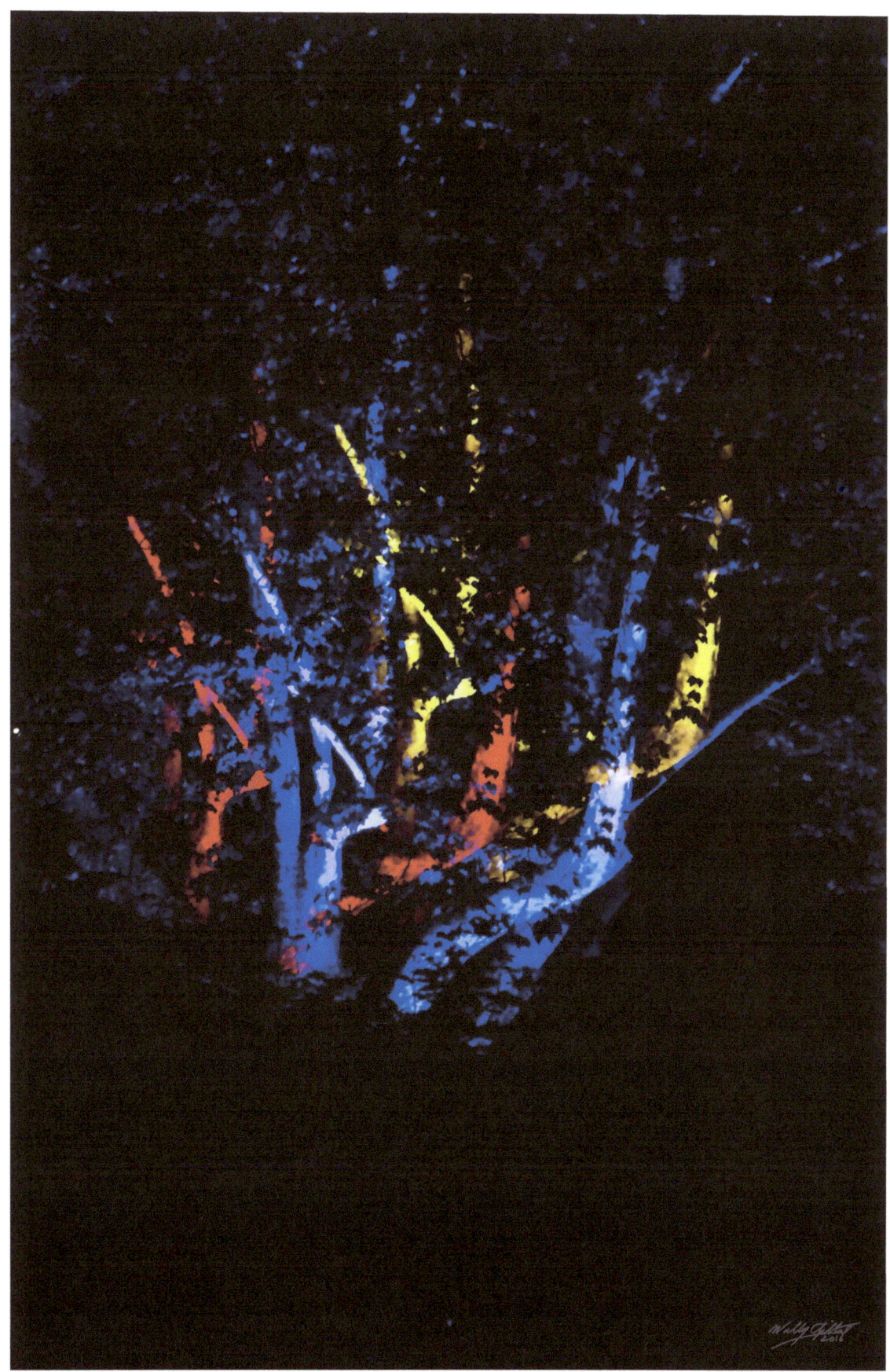

Broken Tree

2016

60" x40"

Printed on Aluminum, edition of 5

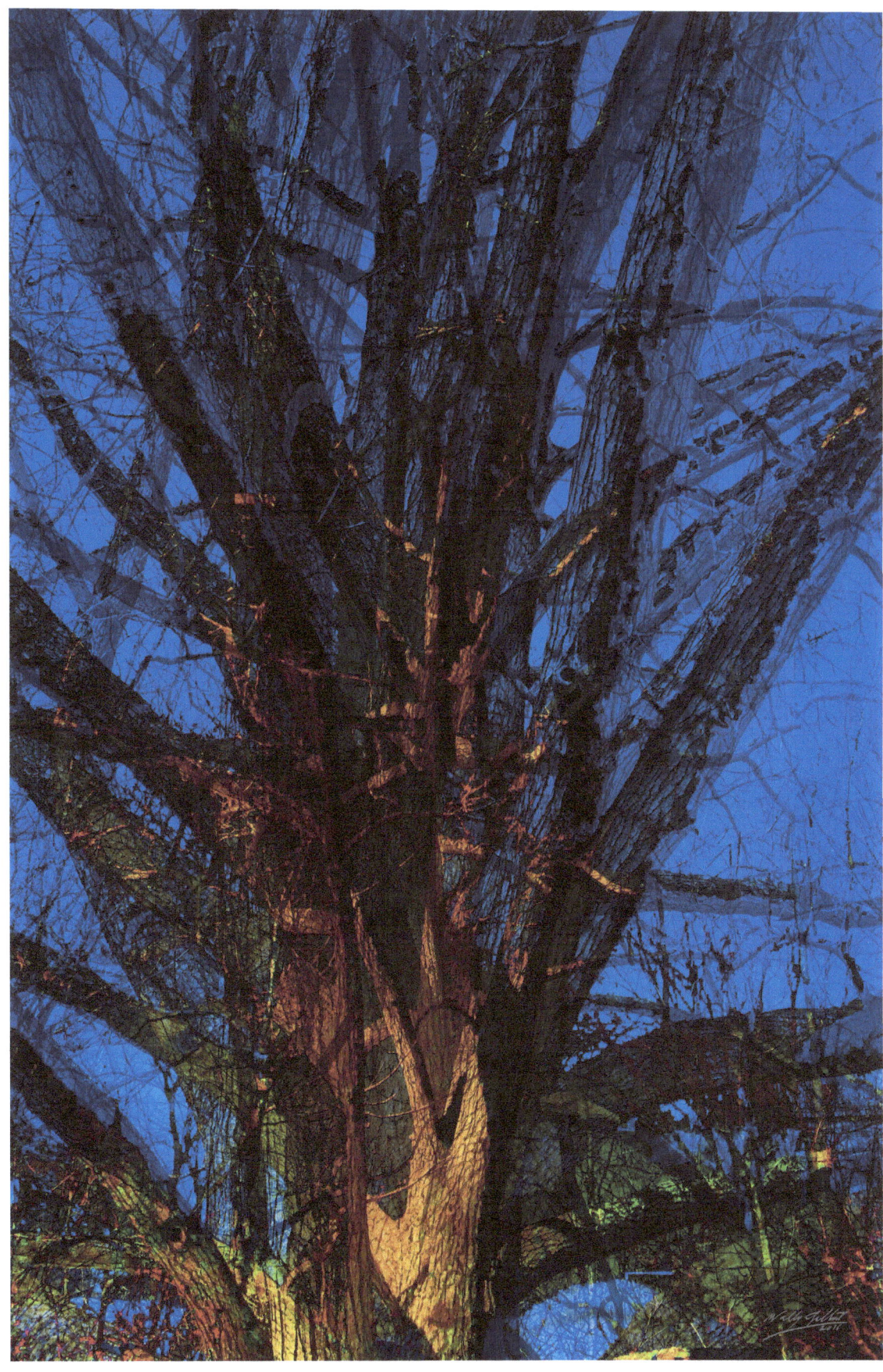

30" x 20" Images

Broken City

2015

30" x 20"

Printed on Aluminum, edition of 5

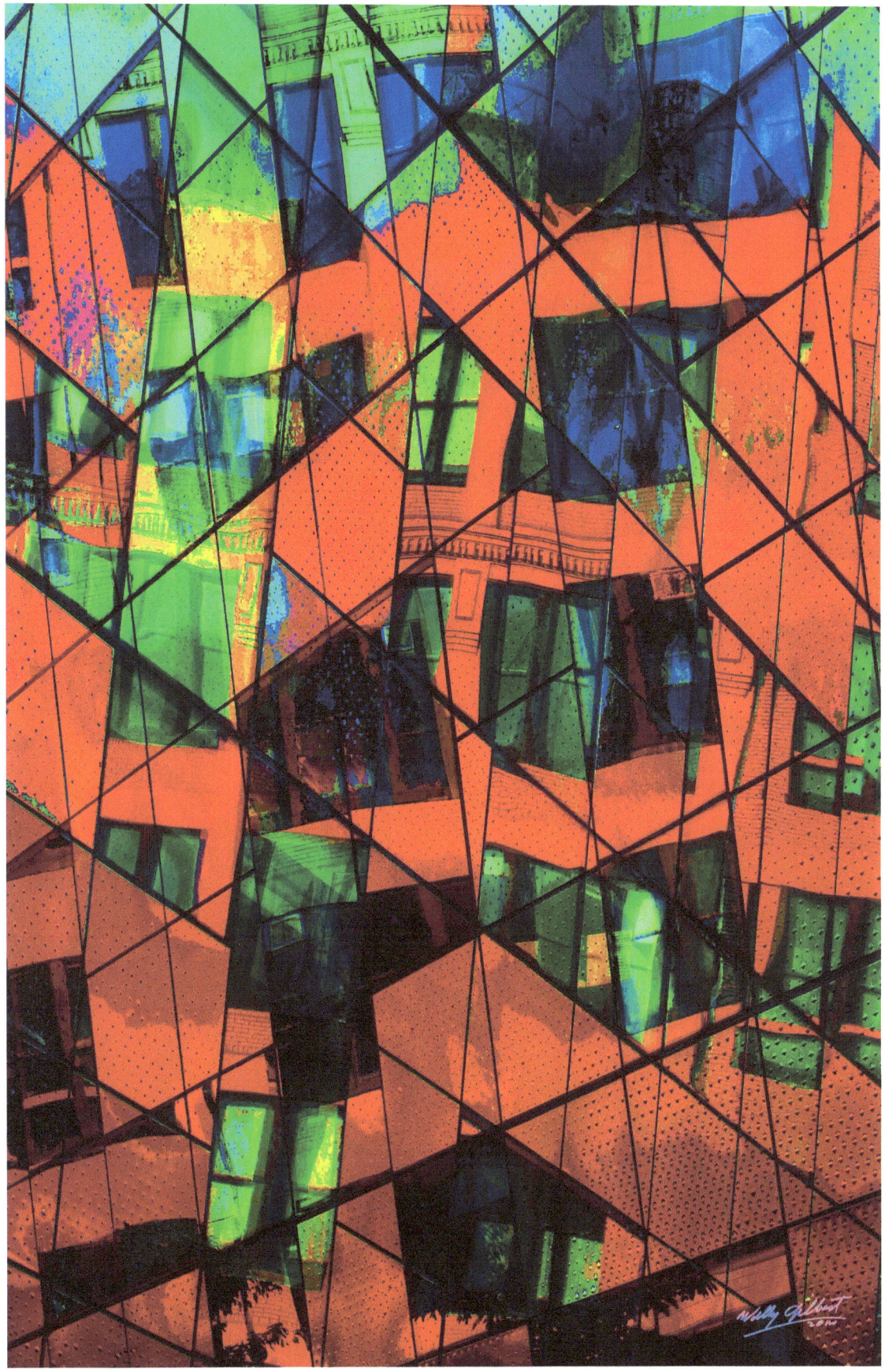

Broken City #2

2015

30" x 20"

Printed on Aluminum, edition of 5

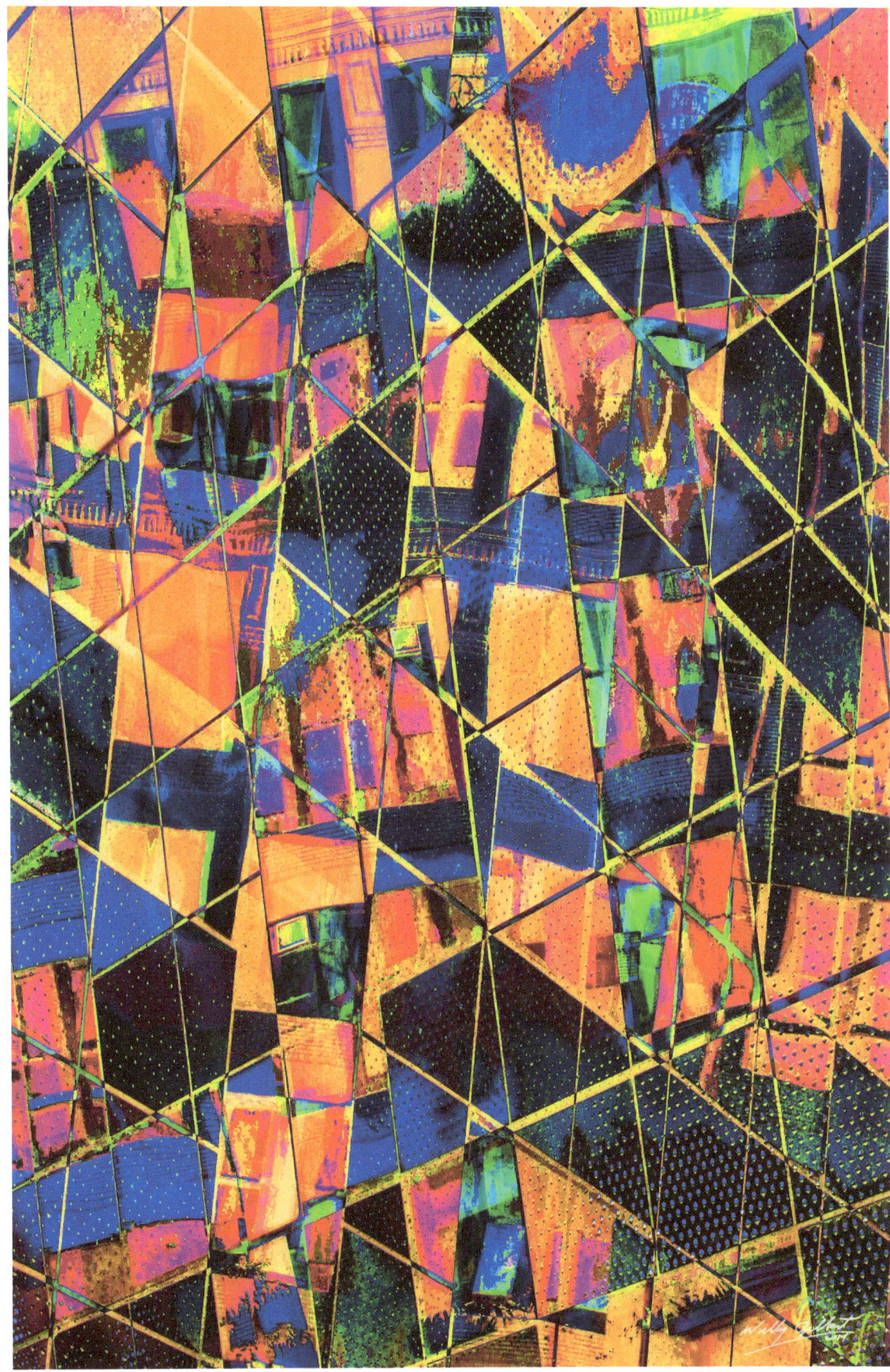

Broken City #3

2015

30" x 20"

Printed on Aluminum, edition of 5

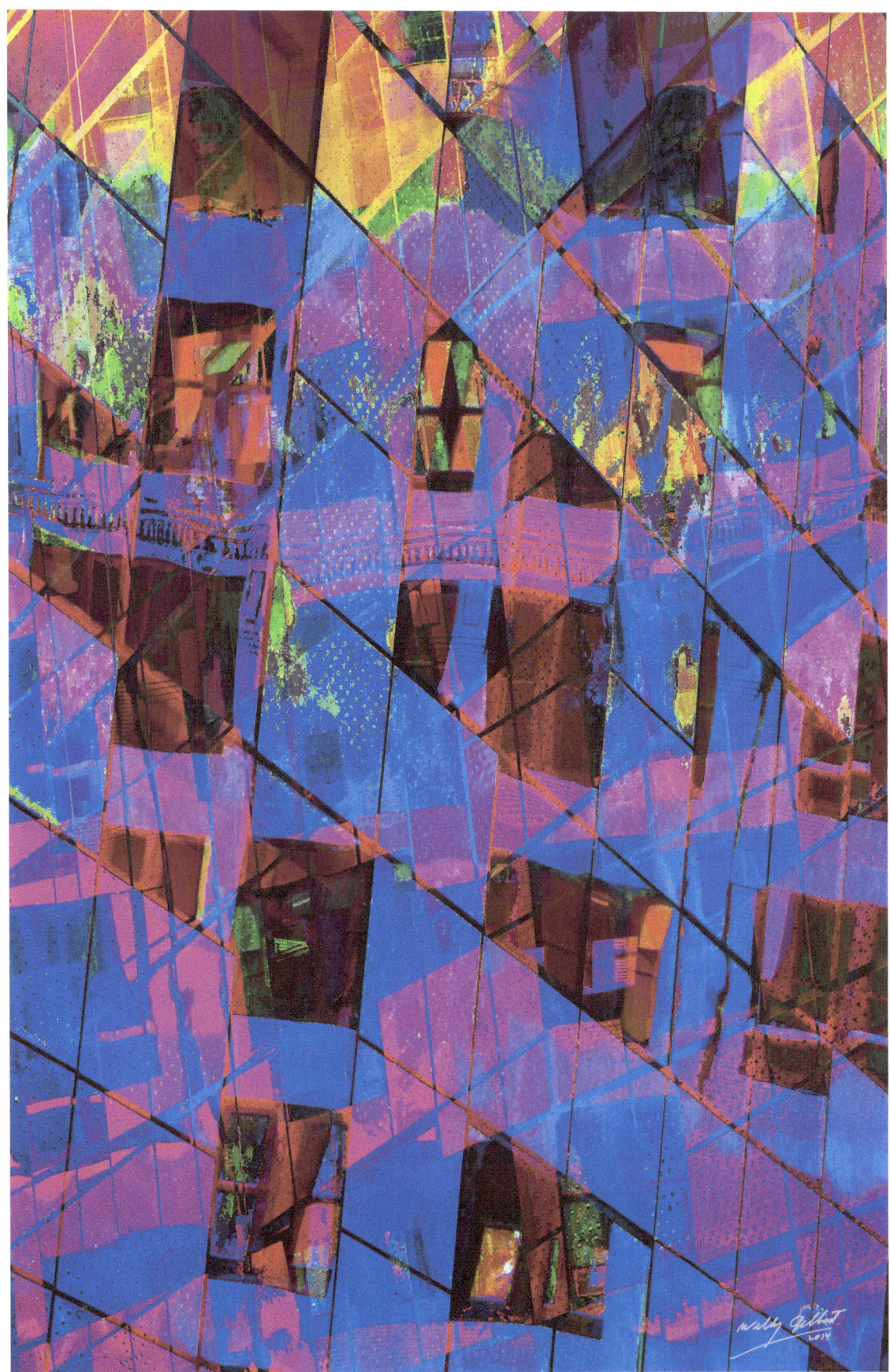

Broken City #7

2015

30" x 20"

Printed on Aluminum, edition of 5

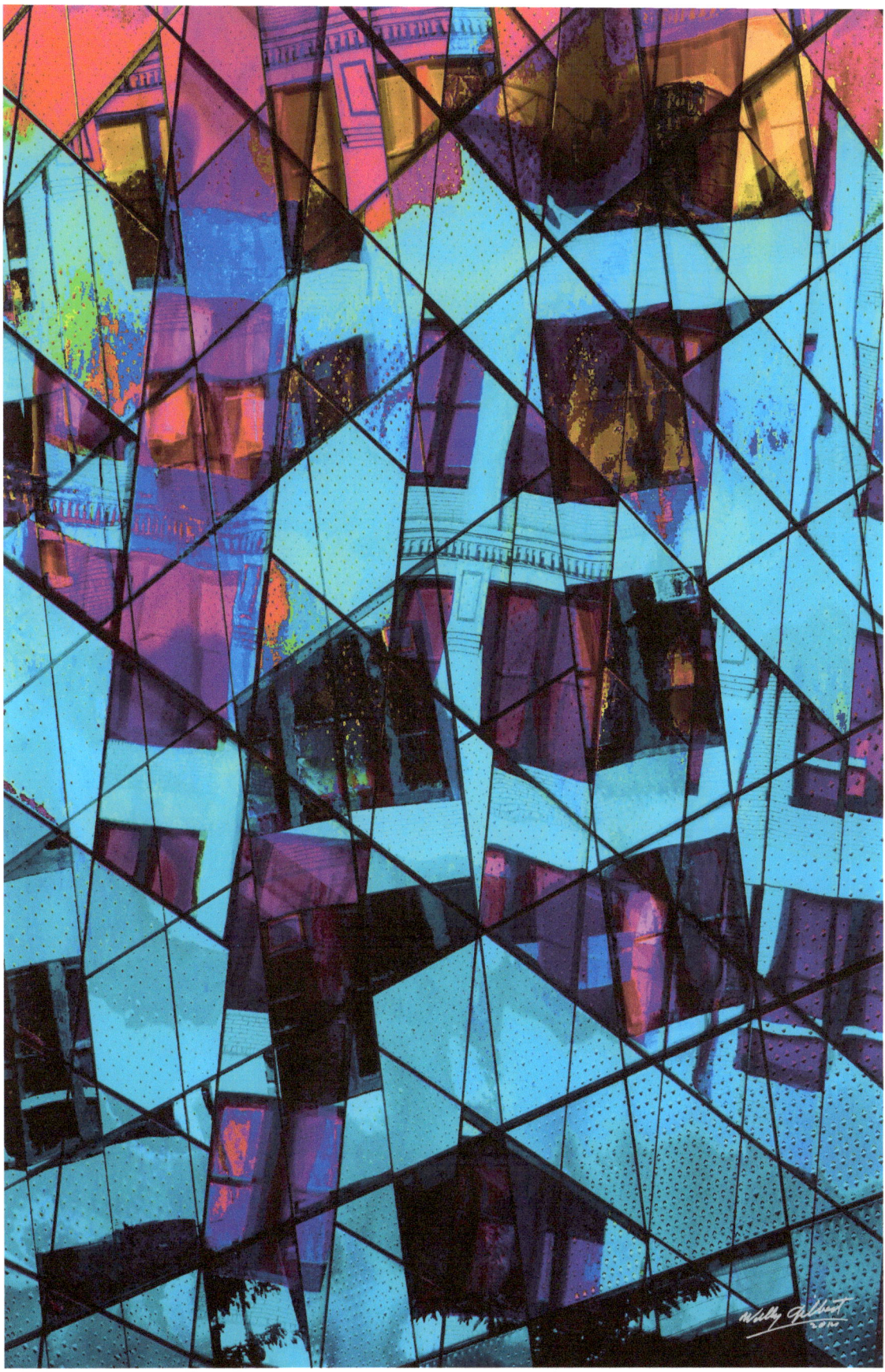

33

Black and White Images

Broken City #2 BW

2016

30" x 20"

Printed on Aluminum, edition of 5

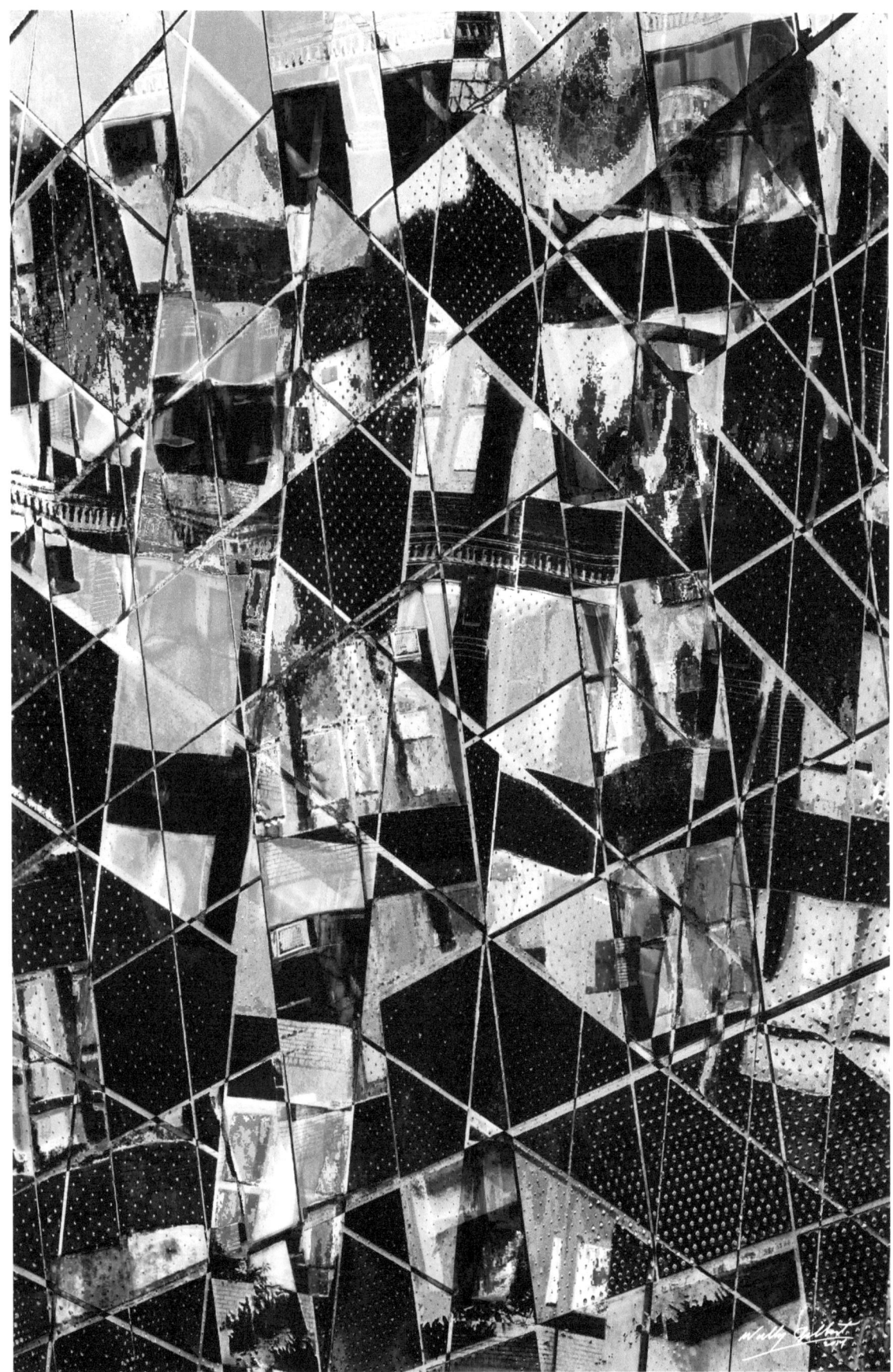

Broken City #5 BW

2016

30" x 20"

Printed on Aluminum, edition of 5

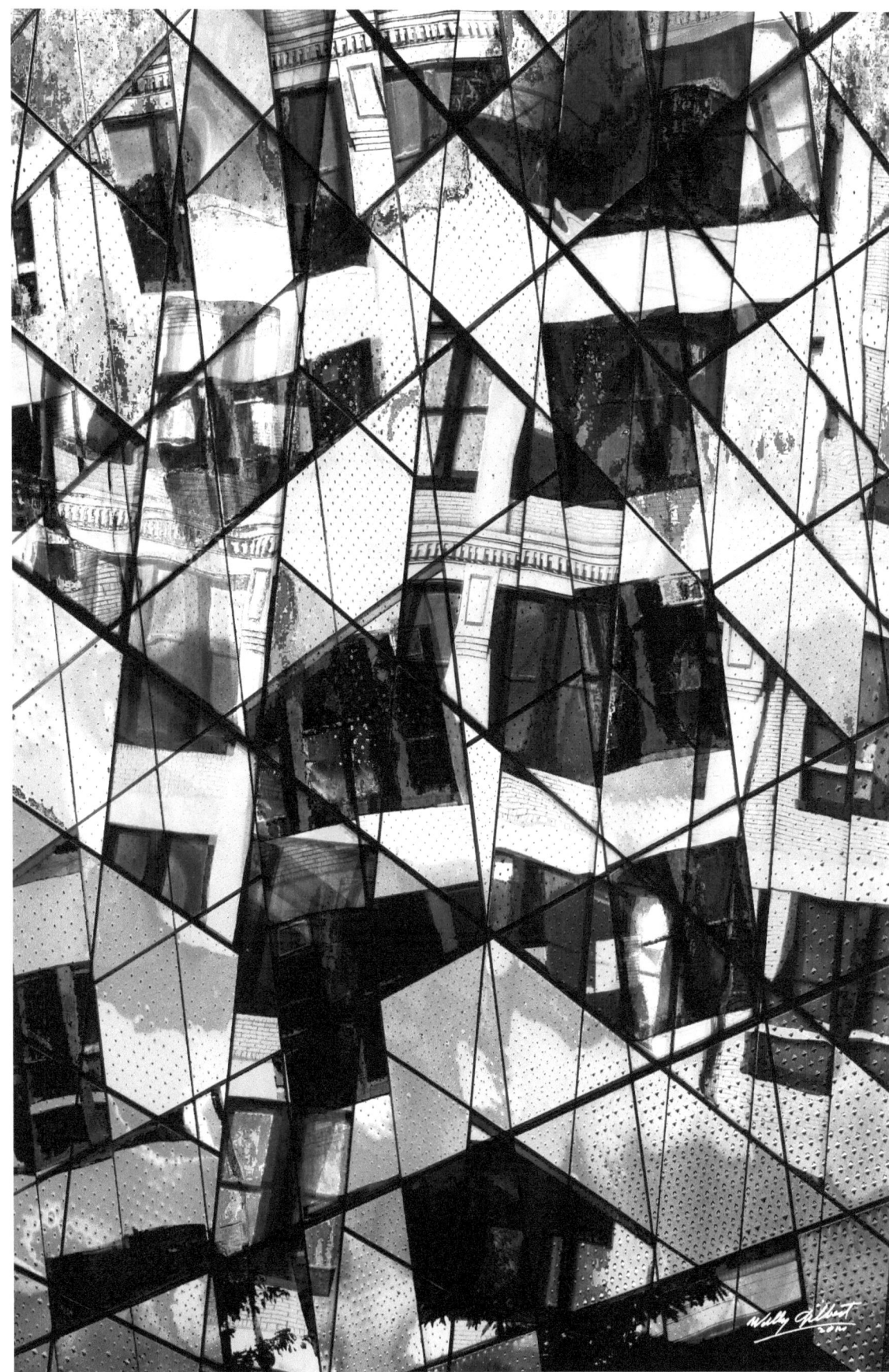

Night Trees – Black and White

2016

30" x 20"

Printed on Aluminum, edition of 5

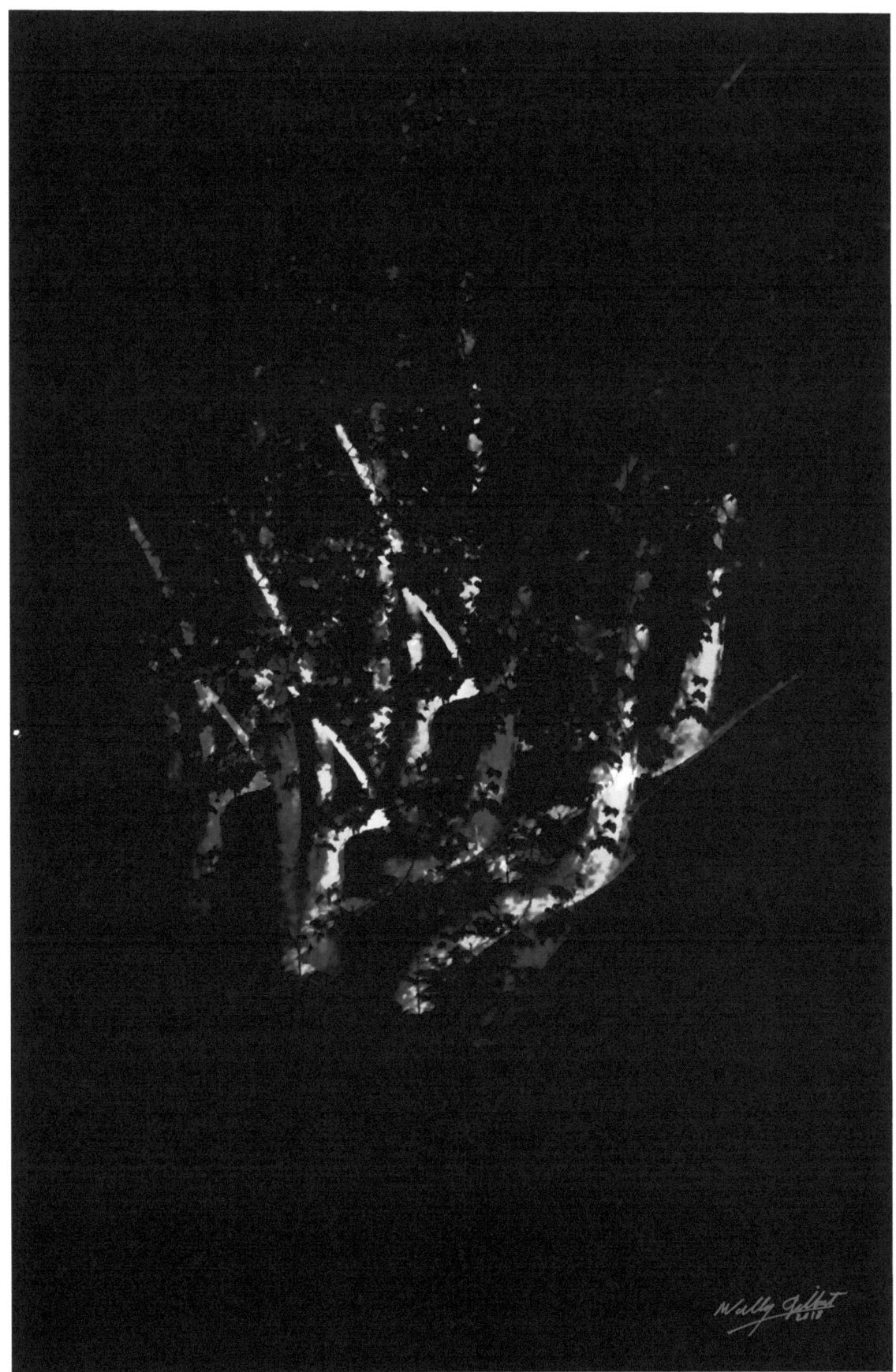

Reflections

2014

30" x 20"

Printed on Aluminum, edition of 5

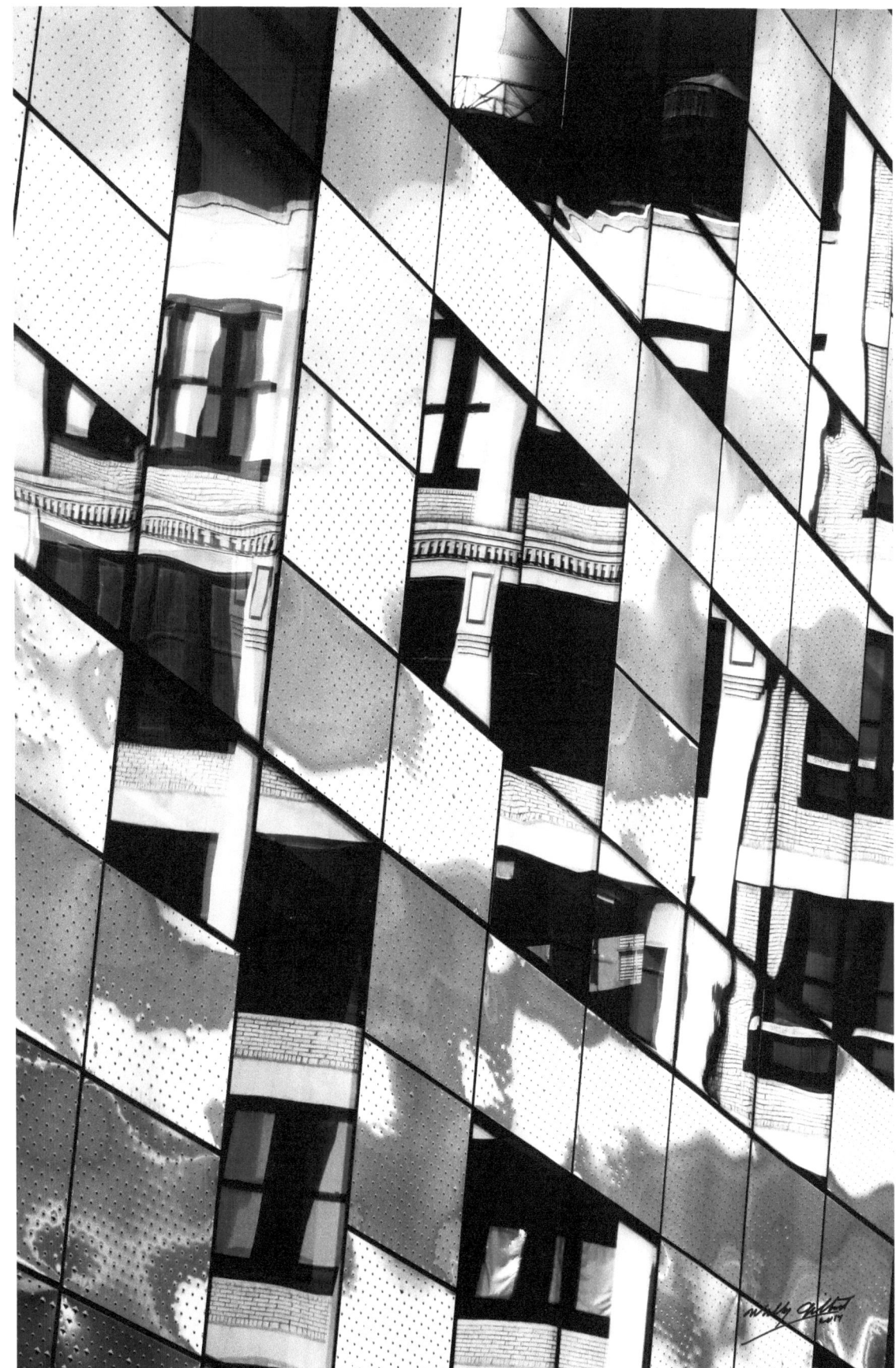

Broken Tree #2

2016

30" x 20"

Printed on Aluminum, edition of 5

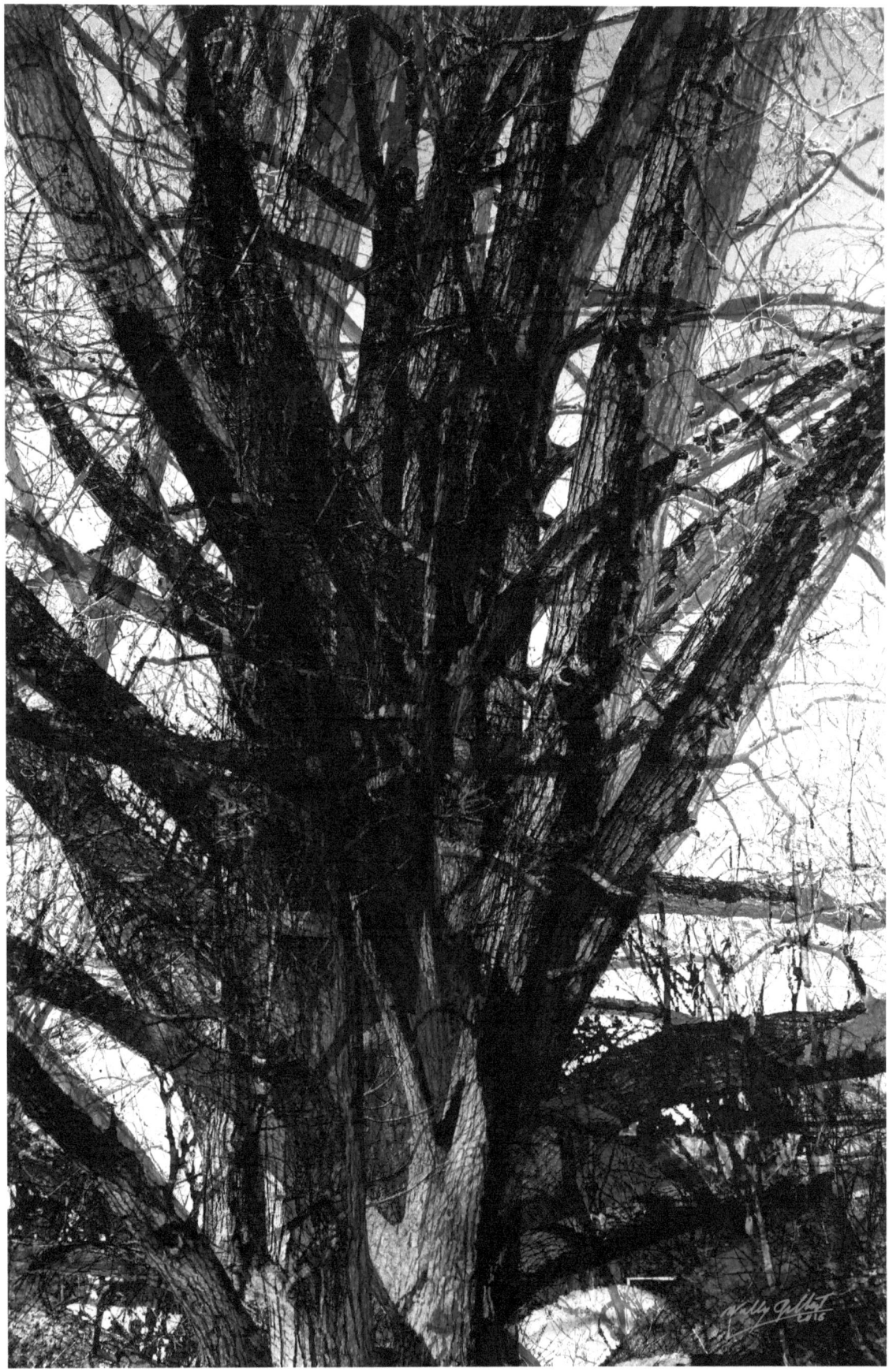

Artist's Statement

I began making digital images as art when I discovered that I could make large prints from images taken with a small digital camera and that these prints carried an emotional and asthetic impact. My earliest work was of fragments of the visual world, either portions of natural scenes or of man's architectural or industrial artifacts. My first one-person show included a 48" x 72" image made from a two mega-pixel camera.

I was invited to Poland, to do an installation at the Norblin Site in Warsaw, by Jan Kubasiewicz and Josef Piwkowski. These photographs of decaying machinery were installed in Warsaw in the Summer of 2007 as twenty-six 12' x 8' hangings and thirty 36" x 24" prints, face-mounted on plexiglas. This show was exhibited again in Lodz and in Poznan.

After photographing dancers in the ballet, I went on to explore abstractions, first in a "Vanishing" series, that was based on a natural form, the outline of a human head. The many patterns produced in that series all shared some aspect of a biological or natural curve, which still was manifest even in the smallest cropping of those images.

In my later work the basic element is a straight, shaded line, which I used to create geometric patterns. The "Geometric Series" explored patterns in color or black-and-white created from overlapping squares or triangles or just from lines, taken either simply or in intersecting groups.

I make many images by hand on the computer. The computer simply holds the intermediate forms as I superpose the many layers I create to build up the image. The images begin in black and white, and then I color them in the computer. I generate these colors either by accessing the colors available or, in a more complicated fashion, by using the ability to change the global input-output functions for each color and intensity separately. When the layers containing the colored images interact with each other, still more color patterns appear. The computer is a digital workspace, driven by my hand and eye.

My most recent work involves photographs moved to extreme values in color space yielding strange color contrasts further superimposed on eachother. These images exemplify my delight in light and form, and my search for a three-dimensional effect on a two-dimensional surface. I search for depth beyond the picture plane and for mystery.

Wally Gilbert's Biography

Wally Gilbert had a long international career as a scientist, working in Molecular Biology on genes and DNA. He was awarded a Nobel Prize in Chemistry, in 1980, for solving the mystery of DNA sequencing. Fred Sanger in England and Gilbert in the United States shared that prize for finding ways to decipher the order of chemical groups along the DNA molecule and hence to make it possible for the first time to read the genes. Those discoveries drove the development of Biology as a gene-based science across the last three decades and led to the working out of the Human Genome program and the current understanding of all organisms.

For the last ten years Gilbert has been working in Digital Art. He began by making large images of fragments of the world, focusing on form, texture, and color, using a small digital camera. Very often these pictures were drawn from machines or from architecture. Jan Kubasiewicz, a professor at the Massachusetts College of Art, saw his work and organized his first one-person exhibition in 2004. He was invited to Poland, by Kubasiewicz and Jozef Zuk Piwkowski, to create an installation at the Norblin Site in Warsaw, an old decaying factory. This installation, consisting of twenty-six 12' by 8' hangings and thirty 36" x 24" prints face-mounted on Plexiglas, was installed at Norblin in Warsaw for two months in 2007 and then later that year in Łodz and again in Poznan in 2009. The set of thirty face-mounted prints were also exhibited in New York, Washington D.C., Los Angeles, and San Diego.

Gilbert was invited to participate in creating a book on the Boston Ballet Company. He spent several years photographing ballet dancers in rehearsal. and These pictures, which capture the joy and motion of the dancers, appeared in a book on that company "Behind the Scenes at Boston Ballet" by Christine Temin with 68 pictures by Wally Gilbert.

Gilbert then moved to abstractions, first based on silhouettes derived from photographs, then to ever more abstract images based on the human head, first still interpretable, but then moving to patterns having only a slight residual aspect of a biological curve. Then he created digital images, made by hand on the computer, based on geometrical forms. This work involved patterns of superimposed shrinking squares and triangles, strongly colored or in black and white, and led finally to images involving single lines. More recently he has been exploring abstractions created by superimposing several photographic images.

"Broken City," Khaki Gallery, Boston, MA   2016

"Patterns & Recognition," Seoul National University Bundang Hospital,
      curated by Chang and Jae Kim   2015-2016

"Transformations," Viridian Artists, Chelsea, NYC   2014

"Patterns & Recognition," The Howard Hughes Medical Institure, Janelia Farm, VA   2014

"Wally Gilbert," CJ Gallery, Art San Diego 2013, San Diego, CA   2013

"Wally Gilbert: A Room of Light," Milton Art Museum, Canton, MA   2013

"Wally Gilbert: Black & White," Khaki Gallery, Boston, MA   2013

"Digital Constellations," Lindau City Museum, Lindau, Germany   2013

"Wally Gilbert: New Black and White Images," Viridian Artists, Chelsea, NYC   2013

"Wally Gilbert", CJ Gallery, Art San Diego 2012, San Diego, CA   2012

"En-Lighten," Khaki Gallery, Boston, MA   2012

"Journeying," The Artemis Gallery, Krakow, Poland,
      curated by Wieslawa Piotrowska-Sowadska   2012

"Pattern & Recognition," The Art Gallery, Antelope Valley College, Lancaster, CA   2012

"Squares, Triangles, and Lines," Galerie im Einstein, Berlin   2011

"Projekt Norblin," New Art Wet Music Foundation, Bydgoszcz, Poland   2011

"Squares and Triangles," Viridian Artists, Chelsea, NYC   2011

"Vanishing," CJ Gallery, San Diego, CA   2010

"Vanishing Profiles," Khaki Gallery, Boston, MA   2010

"The Norblin Project and Other Images," CJ Gallery and OCIO DESIGN GROUP, San Diego,CA   2010

"Wally@Wainwright," Wainwright Bank, Cambridge, MA   2010

"Vanishing," BAAK Gallery, Cambridge, MA   2009

Norblin Installation, Poznan, Poland, curated by Jan Kubasiewicz and Zuk Piwkowski   2009

"The Norblin Project and other Images," CJ Art Gallery, San Diego, CA   2009

"IN COLOR & BEYOND," Khaki Gallery, Boston, MA   2009

"Fresh Fruit," Mayyim Hayyim Gallery, Newton, MA   2009

"Stillness and Motion," Viridian Artists, Chelsea, NYC   2008

"LEEKS & CHAINS," Khaki Gallery, Wellesley, MA   2008

"The Norblin Project and other Images," CJ Art Gallery, San Diego, CA   2007

BAAK Gallery, Cambridge, MA   2007

Norblin Installation, Galeria PATIO,Lodz, Poland,
      curated by Zuk Piwkowski, Jan Kubasiewicz, and Aurelia Mandziuk   2007

Norblin Site Installation, Warsaw, Poland, curated by Jan Kubasiewicz and Zuk Piwkowski   2007

"The Norblin Project: Images of Decay," American Center for Physics, College Park, MD   2007

"IN COLOR," Khaki Gallery, Wellesley, MA   2007

"The Norblin Project: Images of Decay," LACDA, Los Angeles, CA   2006

"The Norblin Project: Images of Decay," Viridian Artists, Chelsea, NYC   2006

Jock Colville Hall, Churchill College, University of Cambridge, Cambridge, UK   2006

Ann Janss Gallery, Los Angeles, CA   2005

Doran Gallery, Massachusetts College of Art, Boston, MA, curated by Jan Kubasiewicz   2004

Wally Gilbert is represented by:

CJ Art Gallery
10755 Scripps Poway Parkway, Suite #542
San Diego, CA 92131
tel. 619.850.7989
email. info@cjartgallery.com

Khaki Gallery
460 Harrison Avenue, Boston, MA 02118
9 Crest Road, Wellesley, MA 02482
tel. 781-237-1095   tel. 781-572-7263

Viridian Artists
548 W 28th Street, sixth floor
New York, NY 10001
tel. 212-414-4040